My C Words

Consultants

Ashley Bishop, Ed.D.
Sue Bishop, M.ED.

Publishing Credits

Dona Herweck Rice, *Editor-in-Chief*
Robin Erickson, *Production Director*
Lee Aucoin, *Creative Director*
Sharon Coan, *Project Manager*
Jamey Acosta, *Editor*
Rachelle Cracchiolo, M.A.Ed., *Publisher*

Image Credits

cover Eric Isselée/Shutterstock; p.2 Eric Isselée/Shutterstock; p.3 Tereshchenko Dmitry/Shutterstock; p.4 CrackerClips/Shutterstock; p.5 GRAPIX/shutterstock; p.6 Tatiana Popova/Shutterstock; p.7 Supertrooper/Shutterstock; p.8 Alexander Raths/Shutterstock; p.9 Masalski Maksim/Shutterstock; p.10 Elena Elisseeva/Shutterstock; back cover Elena Elisseeva/Shutterstock

Teacher Created Materials

5301 Oceanus Drive
Huntington Beach, CA 92649-1030
http://www.tcmpub.com
ISBN 978-1-4333-2547-2
© 2012 Teacher Created Materials, Inc.

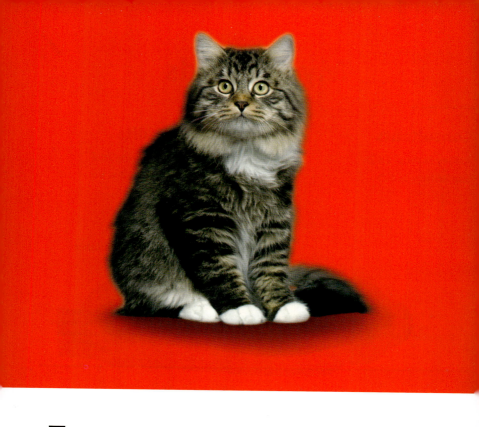

I see a cat.

I see a coat.

I see a **c**up.

I see a car.

I see a computer

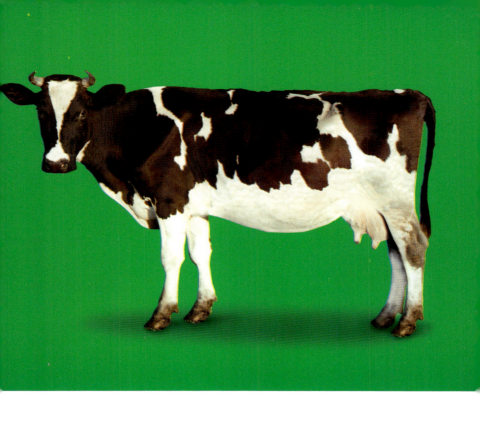

I see a **c**ow.

I see a **c**ook.

I see a camera.

I see a **c**ake.

Glossary

Sight Words

I see a

Activities

- Read the book aloud to your child, pointing to the *c* words as you read them. After reading each page, ask, "What do you see?"
- Have your child use a camera to take a picture of some of the objects that you have around the house that begin with the letter *c*.
- Bake a cake and have your child write the letter *c* on the top with frosting.
- Have your child find the letter *c* on the keyboard of the family computer, a telephone, or a computer at the library.
- Help your child think of a personally valuable word to represent the letter *c*, such as *cat*.